W9-AOX-114

Diabetes

UNDERSTANDING
ILLNESS

Diabetes

Elaine Landau

TWENTY-FIRST CENTURY BOOKS

A Division of Henry Holt and Company
New York

Twenty-First Century Books
A Division of Henry Holt and Company, Inc.
115 West 18th Street
New York, NY 10011

Henry Holt ® and colophon are trademarks of
Henry Holt and Company, Inc.
Publishers since 1866

Published in Canada by Fitzhenry & Whiteside Ltd.,
195 Allstate Parkway, Markham, Ontario, L3R 4T8

Library of Congress Cataloging-in-Publication Data
Landau, Elaine.
Diabetes / Elaine Landau. — 1st ed.
p. cm. — (Understanding illness)
Includes bibliographical references and index.
1. Diabetes—Juvenile literature. [1. Diabetes. 2. Diseases.]
I. Title. II Series: Landau, Elaine. Understanding illness.
RC660.5.L36 1994
616.4'62—dc20   94-13845
                                                                      CIP
                                                                      AC
ISBN 0-8050-2988-5
First Edition 1994

Printed in the United States of America
All first editions are printed on acid-free paper ∞.
10 9 8 7 6 5 4 3 2 1

Photo Credits
p. 13: Billy E. Barnes/Transparencies; pp. 17, 30: Terry Wild Studio;
p. 20: Visuals Unlimited/Hank Andrews; p. 24: Bob Stanley/*Palm
Beach Post*; pp. 29, 53: Shelly R. Harrison/Light Sources Stock; p. 31:
Can Am Care Corporation; p. 35: Visuals Unlimited/D. Newman; p.
37: H. Armstrong Roberts; p. 40 (top): Visuals Unlimited/Arthur R.
Hill; p. 40 (bottom): Visuals Unlimited/Mark E. Gibson; p. 45: Frances
M. Roberts; p. 47: Caroline Wood/F–Stock Inc.

For Lois Kallas

CONTENTS

Diabetes

CHAPTER ONE

What's the Matter with Michelle?

Michelle Blake (name changed) is an attractive, intelligent 13-year-old who enjoys both school and sports. She'd always been healthy, which is why her parents became concerned when she started to mysteriously lose weight. After their daughter dropped more than 25 pounds (11 kilograms) in less than a month, Mrs. Blake took Michelle to a doctor.

Following the medical exam, the doctor told both mother and daughter that he couldn't find anything wrong with Michelle. He also did not order further tests or refer Michelle to a specialist. Instead the doctor spoke at length about how common eating disorders are among young teens. Mrs. Blake and her daughter left his office feeling that the doctor didn't believe Michelle when she told him that she hadn't been dieting. And upon leaving the doctor, they were as perplexed as to what was really wrong with her as they had been when they arrived.

In time Michelle's health worsened and other symptoms appeared. She often felt exhausted, was frequently thirsty, and needed to urinate often. Some days Michelle became nauseous and vomited.

Concerned about her daughter's health, Mrs. Blake brought her to a larger medical facility. There Michelle was examined and a throat culture taken. At that point the doctor she saw thought Michelle probably had strep throat. Everyone in the area seemed to have the flu that winter and a number of young people were being treated at the clinic for it. But until the test results confirmed his diagnosis, Michelle was simply advised to rest and drink plenty of fluids.

The young teen followed the doctor's instructions, but didn't improve. She sipped sodas and fruit beverages throughout the day, yet it was hard for her to keep them down. And as Michelle became dehydrated, dark circles appeared beneath her eyes.

Soon afterward, the throat culture Michelle took confirmed that she had strep throat. Penicillin was pre-scribed but she threw up the pills. Michelle needed to urinate more than ever and although she was frequently tired, she found it hard to sleep. At times Michelle's whole body ached.

One night after she finally fell asleep the young girl's mother noticed that Michelle wasn't resting com-fortably. Her breathing had a rattling sound to it and her skin looked grayish. When at about two o'clock in the morning her mother was unable to wake Michelle, she became concerned. The girl's hands and legs had stiff-ened and her bed was soaked with sweat. Realizing that her daughter needed emergency medical attention, Mrs. Blake dialed 911 for an ambulance. The paramedics arrived within minutes and Michelle was taken to the hospital.

Unfortunately the young teen nearly died that night. Although her family and physicians hadn't known it, Michelle was actually suffering from a chronic and often misunderstood illness. She had diabetes. After arriving at

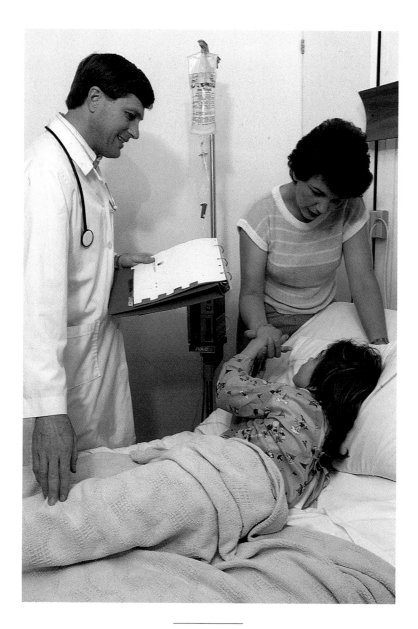

*While medical emergencies involving diabetes
can be frightening, at times the quick reactions
of hospital personnel have saved patients' lives.*

the hospital Mrs. Blake was told that her daughter had developed an emergency condition called diabetic ketoacidosis. The girl's blood sugar level was dangerously high and at first the medical staff wasn't sure they could save her. But, after six hours of intensive efforts it looked as though she'd survive.

Following her recovery Michelle told her friends and family that she was afraid to sleep at night for fear of slipping back into a coma. However, now her doctors knew what the problem was and Michelle was being properly treated for it. She soon found that she could live an active and enjoyable life.

Although Michelle's experience may not be typical of most people with diabetes, such emergencies do occur. When worsening symptoms have gone unrecognized or been ignored, some people have even died. That's what happened to a 23-year-old athletic coach who had lived near Michelle. Unaware that he had diabetes, the young man failed to seek immediate medical attention when he mistakenly thought he had the flu. By the time he got to a hospital it was too late.

Unfortunately many children with diabetes have been misdiagnosed as having the flu, a urinary tract infection, or strep throat. In addition, most people do not know enough about the disease to insist that a simple blood test, which would lead to a correct diagnosis, be administered.

Nevertheless, tragedies can be prevented by becoming knowledgeable about the illness. It's estimated that while nearly 14 million Americans have diabetes, a sizable portion of them don't know it yet. It's important that everyone learn about diabetes, and that's what this book is all about.

CHAPTER
T W O

Diabetes

There are different forms of diabetes and all involve a hormone called insulin. Insulin is produced by the cells of a gland known as the pancreas, which is located just behind the stomach. Insulin plays an important role in how the body uses food.

The body's cells run on glucose—a sugar manufactured when the carbohydrates we eat are digested. Insulin enables the cells in the bloodstream to absorb and use glucose for fuel. But if the pancreas produces too little insulin or no insulin at all, or if the insulin doesn't act effectively, the person can become diabetic. If left uncontrolled, the disease can result in serious physical consequences.

Diabetes is not contagious; you cannot catch it from someone who has it. At present it is still incurable. However, with proper medication and/or eating and lifestyle changes, the disease can usually be effectively managed.

The various forms of diabetes are described below.

TYPE I

Type I diabetes used to be known as juvenile onset diabetes because it most often strikes young people under 30 years of age. About 10 to 20 percent of all Americans with diabetes have Type I diabetes, amounting to nearly 2.8 million people. Although this form of the illness affects a small percentage of people with diabetes, its effect on the body is often the most severe.

In Type I diabetes the person has either completely stopped making insulin or only makes a very small amount of the hormone. Without insulin the body's cells cannot utilize glucose and remains in a state of starvation, regardless of how much the person eats. Without fuel for energy the body will burn needed fat and muscle.

Most people with Type I diabetes must take insulin on a daily basis. The insulin is injected beneath the skin into the body's subcutaneous tissue. If it were taken orally in pill form, the stomach's digestive juices would destroy the hormone before it worked.

The symptoms of Type I often seem to come on suddenly and in some crisis situations the person's life may even be at risk unless immediate medical attention is sought. Unlike people with Type II diabetes, who tend to be overweight, those with Type I are frequently lean.

The key signs of Type I diabetes are listed below:

- a significant weight loss in a short period of time by someone who isn't dieting,
- excessive urination and drinking,
- irritability,
- nausea and vomiting.

Prior to the discovery of insulin in 1921, people who had diabetes frequently had a short life span. However, the use of insulin combined with an adequate diet and the

*A young girl with diabetes gives
herself an insulin injection.*

correct amount of exercise has allowed them to live out their lives comfortably.

In some cases after beginning insulin shots, a person with Type I diabetes will go into remission. During this period, the individual's pancreas once again secretes insulin and the patient's need for the daily shots disappear. In these instances, the blood sugar level (the amount of sugar in the person's bloodstream) stays within the normal range. Such individuals may feel as though they no longer have the disease, but this isn't so. In fact, this stage of Type I diabetes is sometimes referred to as the "honeymoon period," because it doesn't last. At any time, without warning, the individual's blood sugar level may rise, leaving the person in dire need of insulin.

Anyone who has Type I diabetes must be alert to the medical crises described below that can occur due to their condition.

HYPERGLYCEMIA

Hyperglycemia may result when the person's blood sugar levels are too high and the body doesn't have enough insulin to handle it. It is usually a sign of the disease not being properly controlled. When a person with diabetes becomes hyperglycemic, a condition known as ketoacidosis can occur. That's when the body burns itself for fuel and large quantities of ketones (an end product of digested fat) are released. The surplus ketones create a chemical imbalance within the body that can result in a loss of consciousness and subsequent coma (a continuing state of deep unconsciousness).

Ketoacidosis requires immediate medical treatment. Warning signs of this problem include flushed skin, a fruity odor on the breath, difficulty breathing, nausea and vomiting, extreme thirst, lack of appetite, and abdominal pain.

HYPOGLYCEMIA

Effectively controlling Type I diabetes largely depends on achieving a correct balance of food, exercise, and insulin. While hyperglycemia may result when a person with diabetes' blood sugar level soars, another dangerous condition can occur when the opposite is true. Hypoglycemia, also known as low blood sugar or an insulin reaction, appears when the blood sugar level significantly drops. In a person with Type I diabetes it is often the result of too little food, too much exercise, or too much insulin. The physical symptoms of hypoglycemia include irritability, headache, nausea, hunger, weakness, and confusion. Insulin reactions often come on suddenly and are dangerous, since an individual in this condition can slip into unconsciousness. To counteract hypoglycemia the person should take some milk, orange juice, about two packets of sugar, honey, or a sugared soft drink.

TYPE II

Type II diabetes, also known as maturity onset diabetes, is the most common form of the illness. About 80 to 90 percent of Americans with diabetes have this form of the disease. As in Type I, insulin is central to the problem. Those with Type II diabetes usually still produce insulin. However, their bodies may have developed a tendency to store surplus calories as fat as well as build up a resistance to their own insulin's effectiveness. As a result the

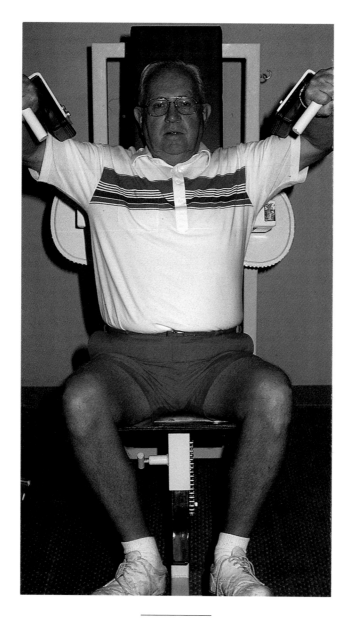

*Excess weight is often a factor
in Type II diabetes.*

insulin fails to do its job and the person's blood sugar level is elevated, creating serious health problems.

While Type I diabetes tends to strike younger individuals, people who have Type II are generally more than 30 years of age. Everyone metabolizes (uses) sugar less effectively as they grow older and this can sometimes trigger an inherited tendency toward the illness. The majority of these people are also overweight. Type II diabetes tends to come on slowly and many of its victims may not even realize that they have the illness. Unfortunately, older individuals frequently mistake the early effects of Type II diabetes for the beginning signs of aging, and therefore fail to seek medical attention.

Although at times the symptoms of Type II diabetes are so mild they go undetected, the most common signs of the illness include:

- increased thirst and urination,
- exhaustion,
- nausea,
- blurred vision,
- dry flaky skin,
- skin wounds that are slow to heal,
- tingling or loss of sensation in the hands or feet.

Although the majority of people with Type II diabetes do not require insulin, sometimes their bodies' ability to produce insulin drops to a point at which the injections are needed. Today as many as 25 percent of the people with Type II diabetes take insulin to control their blood sugar levels, and an additional 50 percent take oral drugs to increase insulin production and enhance the way their bodies metabolize sugar.[1]

GESTATIONAL DIABETES

This type of diabetes develops in some women during pregnancy and then disappears after they give birth. However, some research findings strongly suggest that there's a connection between gestational diabetes and the onset of Type II diabetes in later life. Scientists believe that when other risk factors are present, such as a family history of diabetes, the woman's chances of becoming diabetic increase with each pregnancy. In a study of more than 1,000 women at the University of California, San Diego, researchers found that pregnancy raised a woman's chances of developing diabetes by 16 percent after she turned 40.[2] The Juvenile Diabetes Foundation International and the Diabetes Research Foundation further note that 30 to 40 percent of the women who experience gestational diabetes develop Type II diabetes within five to ten years.

GLUCOSE INTOLERANCE

People with glucose intolerance experience problems metabolizing large quantities of carbohydrates. These individuals are thought to be at greater risk of developing diabetes although the majority of them don't. In the past, glucose intolerance was referred to as latent diabetes or borderline diabetes. However, today it is no longer considered a form of the disease.

Regardless of the type of diabetes—no one can afford to ignore this illness. Diabetes can lead to serious and sometimes fatal health problems. Among these are the conditions listed below.

Diabetes increases the risk of heart disease by affecting the blood vessels and heart. The disease also heightens the possibility of numerous physical problems caused by poor circulation.

People with diabetes are more likely to experience nerve damage. The longer the person has the illness, the more likely this is to occur. People with nerve damage resulting from diabetes are also two to six times more likely to have a stroke.

Our feet take more stress than any other part of the body. The feet of a person with diabetes are more vulnerable to infection than other people's, especially when there is poor circulation or nerve damage in the feet. Infections generally occur in individuals more than 40 years old or those who have had the illness for more than a decade. Neglecting foot problems has resulted in between 18,000 and 20,000 amputations annually among people with diabetes.

There's some evidence that people with diabetes are at greater risk of developing periodontal problems—gum disease.

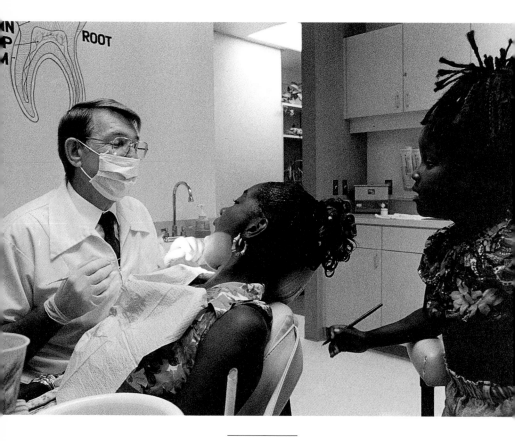

As gum disease is more common among people with diabetes, it is important for them to have regularly scheduled dental checkups.

Diabetes can result in a loss of vision and is presently the leading cause of blindness among adults in North America. Ninety percent of those who have had diabetes for 15 years or more suffer damage to blood vessels in the eye's retina.

Diabetes frequently results in kidney disease. About 30 percent of the kidney-failure patients on dialysis machines have diabetes.

Although the precise cause of diabetes is still unknown, there are several theories about the various factors involved. Studies have shown that there is a hereditary aspect to diabetes. The illness appears to run in some families, so that an individual who has relatives with the disease has a greater chance of developing it. This is especially true for those with Type II diabetes. Research studies have shown that if two people with Type II diabetes have children, most of their offspring will develop the condition. And if an identical twin has Type II diabetes, there's nearly a 100 percent chance that the other twin will have it as well. Yet heredity is frequently less of a factor in Type I diabetes. If two people with Type I diabetes have children, there's only a 20 percent chance that their offspring will be diabetic.

A person's racial or ethnic background may also influence whether or not he or she will develop diabetes. African-Americans, Hispanics, and Native Americans appear to be more vulnerable to Type II diabetes.

Some scientists believe that diabetes may at least partially result from a viral infection that damages the immune system and causes the pancreas to stop making insulin. Stress has also been cited as still another possible factor in the illness's origin. In some instances the stress may be emotional, such as having to deal with the death of a loved one. Other times it may be physical, as in the additional strain placed on the body due to surgery, a severe infection, or a serious accident.

As people age and medical advances enhance life-span expectations, the number of people with Type II diabetes is expected to increase. Presently 18 percent of individuals between 65 and 74 are diabetic. But this number is likely to double within the next 25 years.[3] Undoubtedly, the disease is a force to be reckoned with.

CHAPTER
THREE

Living with Diabetes

"When I first got diabetes at the age of eight, I really thought that the shot I got every day would make it go away," recalled a person with Type I diabetes who's presently in her 40s. "I just couldn't understand that there could be a sickness that my doctor couldn't cure. Now I know better. But it's been a long road—and I have been to many doctors to find the right balance of professional treatment and self care that keep my diabetes under control."[1]

A person with Type I diabetes must learn to effectively manage the illness early on. This generally begins in a doctor's office. After examining the patient and conducting the appropriate tests to arrive at a diagnosis of Type I diabetes, an individualized plan must be devised for the patient. This is necessary to safely balance the patient's insulin, food intake, and exercise level. In creating such a plan the following factors must be taken into consideration:

Age: A person's age will influence his or her needs and lifestyle. For example, management plans for a 7-year-old, a 17-year-old, and a 77-year-old are likely to greatly differ.

Where and How People Spend Their Days: The activity level of a wrestler will not be the same as a file clerk's. A junior high-school student's eating and class schedule will also differ from that of someone working a nine-to-five job or a person who puts off eating to work overtime.

Exercise: The degree to which people with diabetes physically exert themselves, either at work or for health and enjoyment, has a bearing on their food intake and medication.

Diet: How much food people need to sustain themselves as well as the times of day they're able to have a meal or snack must be considered in managing their illness.

Social Environment and Personal Preferences: For a management program to be effective over a period of time, it must be tailored to the patient's needs. If someone takes karate lessons twice a week at his or her usual dinner hour, the plan must allow for it. Although the person might not have time to eat a full meal, a snack might be scheduled instead. The patient's medication might also need to be adjusted to account for the level of physical activity he or she will engage in and the change in diet.

Ideally a Type I management plan should be arranged with the help of a health care team. The team may include the doctor, a nurse-educator, or dietician, and

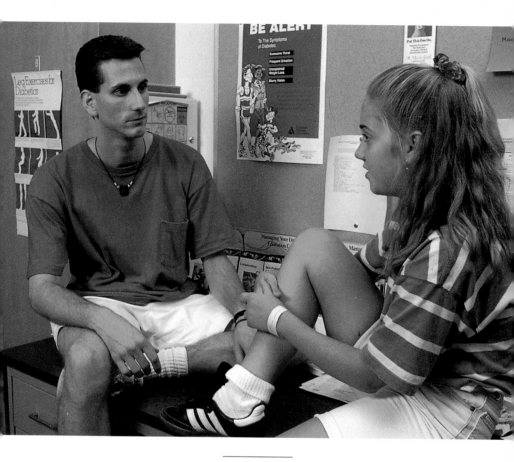

A girl with diabetes is counseled on how to best coordinate her food, exercise, and medication.

any medical specialists such as an eye or foot doctor that might need to be contacted regarding physical problems related to the illness. It's best for a person with Type I diabetes to remain in contact with his or her health care team. As time passes, the team will assist in adjusting the plan during follow-up visits. Trained health care profes-

*A young person with diabetes
monitors her blood glucose level.*

sionals can also pinpoint potential problems that could
turn into crisis situations.

Besides following their management plans, people
who have Type I diabetes must also monitor their blood
sugar, or glucose levels. This is necessary since outside
factors such as excitement, infection, growth periods,
hormonal changes, fatigue, and alcohol and other drugs
can upset the necessary balance. Without monitoring, the
individual will not know there's a problem before physical symptoms appear. In recent years, easy-to-use tests
have been developed to enable people with diabetes to

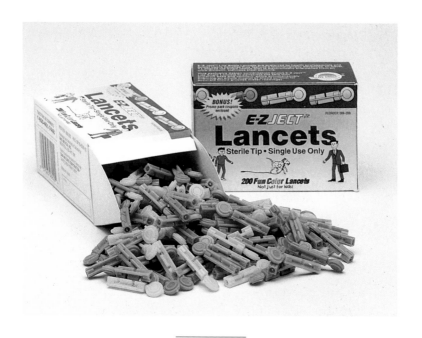

*These colorful Lancets allow young people
with diabetes to easily draw a droplet of blood
for glucose-meter readings.*

monitor their own blood sugar at home or anywhere else
they happen to be.

Self blood-glucose monitoring is an extremely valuable tool for those with diabetes since their blood sugar
levels often quickly change. Many teenagers with diabetes find it especially helpful as it allows them to continue their activities uninterrupted. Prior to going to a
fast-food restaurant with nondiabetic friends, they can
quickly take a blood glucose reading to determine precisely what they can eat.

Knowing their blood sugar levels also helps people

with Type I diabetes determine how much insulin they need. Previously, insulin was generally injected into the body with a syringe, but more recently new methods of delivery have been devised. Today the available options include the following:

Jet Injections: These needleless pressurized jet injectors send insulin through the person's skin in a tiny stream. Some of the new injectors work quite quickly, taking less time to administer insulin than with a standard hypodermic needle.

Insulin Pens: The insulin pen looks like a fountain pen. It is ideal for someone with diabetes who needs insulin while away from home but does not want to take insulin vials and syringes along. The small pen contains everything necessary for an insulin injection.

Insulin Pumps: The insulin pump, which is worn by the person, sends insulin from a storage container through a plastic tube attached to a needle in his or her skin. These devices send a slow trickle of insulin into the body 24 hours a day in an attempt to imitate the action of a well-functioning pancreas. Insulin pumps first became available in the late 1970s. However, today's models are lighter and more compact. They also deliver the insulin more precisely, affording a greater degree of control.

Infuser Methods: These entail planting a needle within the skin that serves as a gateway for the insulin shots.

Even though people with Type I diabetes may learn to advantageously use insulin, they still must choose their foods wisely. In the past, people with diabetes were encouraged to eat high-protein, meat-based meals. Bread, potatoes, and other starches were only permitted in small portions. Although they could eat vegetables, at the time these foods were not considered to be particularly useful in lowering blood sugar levels.

However, following substantial research, this thinking changed. Today the American Diabetes Association (ADA) recommends a diet that is low in fat and high in fiber and complex carbohydrates. Complex carbohydrates, such as peas, brown rice, and cereals, act to raise sugar levels gradually and are often nutritionally valuable. Complex carbohydrates differ from less desirable food such as cakes, danishes, and candy, which contain simple carbohydrates that rapidly raise blood glucose levels and aren't rich in vitamins and nutrients.

Healthful eating habits for people with diabetes also involve staying away from foods that are high in fats and cholesterol. Among these are fried chicken, creamy soups and sauces, fatty meats, and thick gravies. Ice cream, butter, and whole-milk cheeses should be avoided while frozen yogurt, margarine, and skim-milk products can be substituted. Refined sugar should be used rarely as a special treat or as an emergency response to an insulin reaction. People with diabetes should carefully read labels when purchasing food. Many frozen packaged foods contain large "hidden" amounts of sugar, as do condiments such as ketchup, some mustards, and relishes.

The times of the day at which people with diabetes eat and the quantity of food eaten can sometimes be as important as the foods themselves. To help control their blood glucose levels, ideally such individuals should have small portions of a variety of nutritious nonfatty foods. Two food plans, the Exchange Group System and the British Diabetic Association System, have been developed to help people with diabetes plan healthy meals.

The importance of diet cannot be underestimated in the prevention and control of diabetes. This was emphasized by Dr. Denis Burkitt, an English physician who spent much of his life practicing medicine in underdeveloped countries. As he said of the relationship between diet and diabetes, "Everyone used to say, 'Oh diabetes is due to genetics. You can get mice to all have diabetes. . . . There is a genetic element, but the genes only cause the disease in a certain environment. We can alter our environment, but we can't alter our genes.'

"As an example of this there's a little island in the Pacific way out east of Borneo, called Nauru. . . . In the early 1950s there was hardly any Type II diabetes there as in the other Pacific Islands." However, after several industrialized countries invested in the island, the native people increasingly took on the habits and customs of the more modernized Western nations. Burkitt described what happened this way: "They gave up eating the island food they had traditionally adopted. And instead they began importing hamburgers, cola drinks, french fries, and what have you. Twenty years or so later, over 40 per-

The fruits of the prickly pear were a valued and healthful staple of the Pima Indians' diet.

cent of the entire population of Nauru over the age of 20, male and female, are diabetics."[2]

A similar instance occurring closer to home involves the Pima Indians of the Southwest United States. At one time these Native Americans largely existed on what grew in their desert habitat and enjoyed remarkably good health. Their diet included things like the edible sprouts of the bloodroot, acorns, fruits of the prickly pear, tepary beans, wolfberries, mesquite pods, and mustard seeds.

However, in the 1940s the situation began to change. While at times some of these Native Americans still ate desert plants and wild game, for the most part they switched to a mainstream American diet. Foods such as processed white bread, instant pudding, hamburgers, and french fries were especially popular as were a wide assortment of junk food snacks and desserts.

By the 1970s nearly 40 percent of the Pima Indians

more than 35 years of age had developed Type II diabetes. Unfortunately the problems continued and by the 1990s about half the Pimas within that age range had diabetes— the highest rate known internationally. Sadly a number of other Native American groups are not far behind.

Studies of the population revealed that while many of the Pimas were genetically predisposed to diabetes, the disease hadn't surfaced in the past due to their healthy eating habits. Botanists carefully analyzing the original foods of the Pimas' found that acorns and mesquite pods rank among the top 10 percent of foods in controlling blood sugar. Other former Indian staples were beneficial as well.

Today medical specialists hope that a return to at least some of the Pimas' foods of the past will be helpful in combating this problem. As one researcher stressed, "For Native Americans and other recently Westernized indigenous people, a return to a diet similar to their traditional one is no nostalgic notion. It may, in fact, be a nutritional and survival imperative."[3] Some feel that these age-old staples should be incorporated into the diet of the general public as well.

Although Type I and Type II diabetes are similar in many ways, people with Type II diabetes can often completely control the illness through lifestyle changes. As Dr. Sherman Holvey, former president of the American Diabetes Association, described the best route for people with Type II diabetes: "The doctor may call the shots, but it's the patient who carries the ball. Weight management and exercise will pay off in better health and a longer life."[4]

Experts agree that those who have Type II diabetes

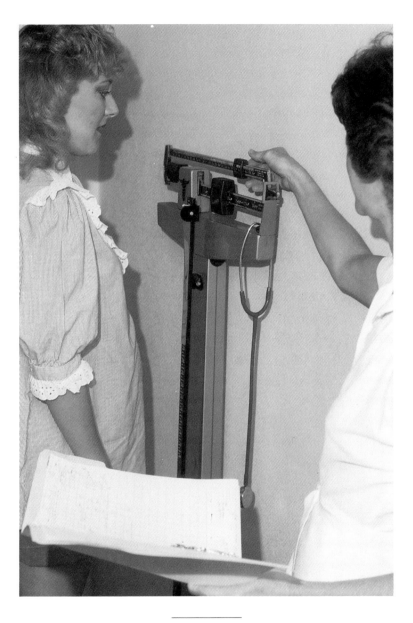

Maintaining a desirable weight is important
in controlling Type II diabetes.

must get in shape in order to shape their future well being. While the food suggestions for those with Type I diabetes are recommended for Type IIs as well, usually Type IIs must also lose weight. In fact, a large number of people with Type II diabetes weigh between 30 and 60 pounds (14 and 28 kilograms) more than they should. Many could actually control their insulin and blood sugar levels simply by losing the extra pounds.

Research has revealed that in some cases even losing 10 pounds (4.5 kilograms) can make a major difference for people who have Type II diabetes. That's because weight loss brings about important physical changes within their bodies. Before long the following beneficial results often occur:

- extremely high insulin levels fall,
- the blood sugar levels of those with Type II diabetes improve,
- muscle tissue that had formerly resisted insulin's effect begins to better utilize sugar.

However, to keep these benefits, people with Type II diabetes must act before the disease has severely affected their bodies. According to diabetes specialist Dr. Robert Henry, "The most dramatic response to even a small weight loss takes place in those who have had diabetes for under five years. With the passage of time, uncontrolled diabetes becomes more difficult to treat through weight loss, and drugs may be necessary. Unfortunately, some Type II diabetics' resistance to insulin becomes so intense that like those with Type I, they need to take insulin as well as medications that enhance the body's insulin production."[5]

Once people with Type II diabetes have reached this point with their weight loss, a vicious cycle sometimes begins. Those who take either insulin or drugs for the illness tend to put on weight more easily than those who don't. That's because insulin acts to store any excess sugar from sweets as fat. And as was noted earlier, extra body fat is detrimental for someone who has Type II diabetes.

Although the solution for most people with Type II diabetes sounds simple enough, more than 95 percent of the people who go on diets to lose weight are unable to maintain that weight loss for an extended period of time. If someone is merely dieting to improve his or her appearance, gaining back the weight may be discouraging—but those who have diabetes face more serious consequences. The American Diabetes Association suggests the following to help individuals with Type II diabetes lose weight and keep it off:

> **Develop a realistic individually tailored weight-loss plan**. This may be best done with the help of a dietician or a nurse-educator. People who set rigid and punishing exercise goals for themselves or try to exist on tasteless foods they dislike are doomed to fail. Those with Type II diabetes require a flexible long-term food plan geared to maintaining their desired weight.

Sheilia Food, R.N., a University of Rochester nutrition and behavior modification specialist, described how to sensibly approach the task as follows: "We figure out exactly what each diabetic needs to do to lose weight, based on their weight and level of activity. I just don't

A low-fat diet and regular exercise are essential for people with Type II diabetes.

say, 'You've got to cut calories.' I say, 'We can cut this T-bone steak down to three ounces and save 300 calories. Are you willing to do that?' I show them that riding a stationary bicycle for 10 minutes burns 60 calories, or that walking one mile burns 60 or 70 calories. We chisel off about 3,500 calories a week [one pound] through diet and exercise. People with diabetes learn that cutting a few calories here and burning a few calories there makes a tremendous difference. It's what puts them in control."[6]

Someone with diabetes who is more than 40 pounds (18 kilograms) overweight and has never successfully lost and kept off the weight might consider going on a medically supervised low-calorie liquid diet. One weight-loss specialist described the benefits this way, "We use [the liquid diet] to initiate weight loss. We might keep someone on it for a month, then gradually bring in foods that allow them to continue to lose weight, or maintain their weight loss."[7]

Be Informed When Choosing Foods. When purchasing products look for labels indicating the food's fat and caloric content. Many so-called diabetic foods are surprisingly high in fat and cholesterol. It's also important to pay attention to the portion size noted. Food values are generally given by portion rather than for the whole package. Some packaged foods that are not labeled "lean," "light," or "dietetic" may actually be less fattening and healthier than specialized diet products. Many canned soups without cream or milk as well as tofu are good choices.

Plan Snacks to Avoid Bingeing. The insulin levels of many people with diabetes peak at about four o'clock in the afternoon. Since insulin stimulates the appetite late afternoon, that may be an especially difficult time for those trying to lose weight to adhere to their diets. Possible bingeing may be avoided by allotting some calories for a nutritious snack at about that time. Pass up buttery pastries and deep-fried foods for fresh fruit and air-popped popcorn.

Avoid Over-the-Counter Weight-Loss Aids. These appetite suppressants often contain the substance phenylpropanolamine, which may be harmful to people with diabetes. Such non-prescription diet pills may help bring on high blood pressure as well as kidney and eye problems in people with diabetes.

Monitor Blood Sugar Levels Regularly. It's essential for people who have Type I diabetes to monitor their blood sugar levels. But many individuals with Type II diabetes don't feel it's necessary for them. However, monitoring blood sugar levels is especially important for those dieters with Type II diabetes because it allows them to see how different eating patterns affect their blood sugar and overall control of the disease.

Another extremely important element in controlling Type II diabetes is exercise. According to Dr. Gerald

Reaven, a Stanford University professor of medicine and an endocrinologist, "Exercise appears to help muscle cells take up and use sugar even when there are lower levels of insulin in the blood."[8] This beneficial effect lasts for up to 48 hours. Exercise is especially important for people with Type II diabetes since their bodies are often unable to effectively use insulin. In addition, exercise burns off excess calories, which assists these individuals with weight control.

While doctors routinely encourage exercise to help control Type II diabetes, scientists have recently found that physical exercise may even be useful in preventing the disease entirely in some patients. Harvard University researchers who followed more than 22,000 male physicians for a five-year period found that those who exercised vigorously at least once a week were 36 percent less likely to develop diabetes. The study further showed that the more an individual exercised, the risk of developing Type II diabetes was lowered.

The results of the study were confirmed by similar independent research projects. These included the Nurses Health Study, which revealed that female nurses who exercised once a week were 33 percent less likely to become diabetic.

Yet for exercise to be beneficial to people with both Type I and Type II diabetes, it's essential that they be aware of the precautions listed below.

People with diabetes should exercise when their blood sugar level is within the normal range. Undertaking vigorous activity when the blood sugar level is too low can result in hypoglycemia. Besides taking his or her blood sugar level prior to exercising, the individual should also do the following:

Carry hard candies or some other readily absorbed form of carbohydrate while exercising in case signs of low blood sugar suddenly appear.

Drink additional liquids or avoid exercising on particularly hot, humid days.

Carry a medical alert card or bracelet identifying the person as a diabetic in case an emergency arises while exercising.

Try to work out at the same time each day. This is important in maintaining the desired balance among insulin, physical activity, and food intake. Someone who isn't used to exercising should not overdo it. It's also important to have a five-minute warm up and cool down period before and after the workout.

Wear comfortable running shoes that fit properly. Since many adults with diabetes experience foot problems, it's important to wear a comfortable, well-cushioned shoe. A study comparing running shoes to street shoes found running shoes superior at preventing blisters on people with diabetes. These well-ventilated mesh shoes also tend to keep feet drier during exercise periods.

A medical alert bracelet can be useful in identifying someone with diabetes in the event of an emergency.

Physical activity was the basis of a new health care program designed for the Zuni Indians of New Mexico. Like a number of other Native American groups, the tribe had developed an exceedingly high rate of Type II diabetes. By the early 1980s more than a third of the Zuni adults were contending with the problem—about seven times that of the United States general population. However, Bruce Leonard, a public-health educator and marathon runner with the Indian Health Service, firmly believed that the people he served could be helped through exercise.

Leonard started out by inviting a group of Native Americans with diabetes treated at the Zuni Public Health Service Hospital to an aerobics class at the high-school gym. But even though more than a dozen patients seemed interested and agreed to come, no one showed up. Leonard spent the evening alone with his tape player and exercise tapes.

The public-health educator knew that weight reduction through exercise might be difficult for some of these Native Americans to accept. The Zuni traditionally believed that a rounded figure was a sign of achievement and success. It supposedly demonstrated that the person did not have to do physical labor. Yet he also knew that the Zunis were concerned about their health and anxious to do what was best for themselves.

Although Leonard contacted the intended participants again, not a single person attended the next six exercise sessions. Then one overweight Zuni woman who had diabetes showed up for the seventh session. She did the aerobics routine and returned for the next class with a friend. Before long a small group of females were regularly attending and enjoying the sessions.

As time passed, others heard that these participants were both losing weight and feeling better. Before long the original group was joined by a number of Zuni males who wanted to reap the benefits of exercise as well. Within six months more classes had to be added for all who wanted to attend.

By 1984 the Zuni Diabetes Project was well under-way. In addition to the exercise classes, the program also included walking and running clubs, a formalized

*Daily physical exercise can be an important
aspect of maintaining an ideal weight.*

weight-loss program, a run-bikeathon, and a summer series of marathons.

The project was extremely successful. Many of the participants lost significant amounts of weight, developed new eating habits, and learned to control their blood sugar. Numerous Zunis either lessened or no longer needed the medication they were taking for their condition.

Some of the Native Americans became exercise instructors, staffing a new tribal Wellness Center. The center offers ongoing exercise classes as well as a gym housing weight-training equipment. Out of a population of 8,546 Native Americans on the Zuni reservation, more than 1,800 are presently involved in exercise programs.

A large number of these individuals have taken up jogging and running. It's fitting that so many Zunis become runners since in ancient times running was an important part of Zuni culture. During a Zuni event known as the stick race, superior Indian athletes of the past displayed their strength and fortitude by running barefoot for more than 25 miles (40 kilometers) through the brush. Many feel that today's Zuni runners would make the stick racers of past generations proud.

The results of programs like the Zuni Diabetes Project have encouraged physicians to more vigorously caution their patients against being couch potatoes. This approach was summed up by Dr. Donnell Etzwiller, president of the International Diabetes Association in Minneapolis, Minnesota, who said, "I think the medical profession has to become more aggressive in this area. We need to start including exercise in our therapeutic prescription."[9]

CHAPTER FOUR

Future Hopes

In recent years diabetes research has been extremely promising. Among the projects underway is the search for an insulin pill to replace injections and other more cumbersome methods. Yet before insulin could be taken in pill form, scientists had to find a way to stop it from being digested in the stomach and small intestine before reaching the bloodstream where it's needed.

To help solve the problem an experimental plastic coating has been created to protect insulin taken daily from the digestive process. This protective covering allows the capsule to reach the large intestine, where the plastic dissolves in the presence of the natural bacteria there. As water enters the large intestine the insulin is then carried into the colon, where it enters the bloodstream.

Having an insulin pill would afford people with diabetes considerable ease and flexibility in taking their medication. The plastic-coated insulin pill has already been successfully tried on diabetic animals at the Medical College of Ohio and may soon be available to humans.

While an effective insulin pill would be welcomed, scientists have also been working to cure the illness.

Some believe that the current treatment for chronic pancreatitis, an inflammatory condition of the pancreas, may hold important answers in their search. Often patients suffering from pancreatitis end up having their pancreas removed. Since the pancreas contains the cells that manufacture insulin, once the organ is taken out the person automatically becomes diabetic, even though he or she may have never had the illness before.

New research suggests that if those vital insulin-producing cells are removed from the pancreas and transplanted back into the patient, that individual will still generate the insulin needed by the body. On May 15, 1990, Marge Heayn of Edmonton, Canada, received such a cell transplant and became the only recipient whose transplant cells functioned for two years following the operation. Unfortunately in August 1992, the cells began to fail, and Heayn had to start taking insulin. Some physicians thought her case demonstrated how far research had come in this area, as well as how far it had to go.

The possibilities are promising, but there are stumbling blocks to overcome. Since the transplant recipients with pancreatitis received their own cells, their bodies did not reject the transplanted tissue. But the situation would be different for people with diabetes desiring transplants. Since their insulin-producing cells don't function adequately, the transplants would have to come from donors and the recipients might reject them.

Scientific teams are actively working to find a way around the problem. As David M. Kendall of the Diabetes Center, Division of Endocrinology and Metabolism at the University of Minnesota, put it, "If that and other hurdles can be overcome . . . this kind of transplantation may be the most appealing and simplest method for restoring normal . . . [cell] function that's been destroyed in many patients with diabetes."[1]

Meanwhile, in various countries throughout the world, doctors are looking into different aspects of diabetes with the hope of improving the lives of people with diabetes as well as finding a cure. Researchers in Toronto, Canada, at the Hospital for Sick Children have found that an element in cow's milk may actually trigger the onset of Type I diabetes in some predisposed individuals. Testing in Norway is also underway to see if excluding cow's milk from babies' diets for a time will provide some degree of protection against the illness. One researcher summed up their hopes for such projects this way, "If we are right, it could be the beginning of the end of diabetes."[2]

In separate clinical trials across America other researchers are exploring how insulin can be used in new ways to suppress diabetes. Low doses of insulin were injected into lean adult mice to see if the hormone would prevent disease symptoms that might surface later on. In an even broader study, researchers in 16 European countries are attempting to learn whether a certain B vitamin can disrupt the body's destruction of beta cells (insulin-producing cells) with the hope of either preventing or delaying Type I diabetes. Since similar research in the United States yielded mixed results, scientists hope a large international study will provide more information.

While efforts to find a cure for diabetes are encouraging, a crucial breakthrough in treating the disease was announced in June 1993, when the results of a project known as the Diabetes Control and Complications Trial were revealed at the annual meeting of the American Diabetes Association. Researchers on the project reported that the most devastating complications of diabetes could be delayed or prevented if people with diabetes carefully monitored their own blood sugar levels throughout the day.

The researchers stressed that these individuals also needed to inject themselves with insulin four to seven times daily to keep their blood sugar at a normal level. Presently many generally do not monitor themselves that closely, and insulin-dependent individuals usually inject themselves just once or twice a day.

The extensive study began in 1983 and was conducted at nearly 30 medical centers across the United States and Canada. Some 1,441 people who had Type I diabetes participated—some hadn't experienced any medical complications as a result of their illness, while others had contended with some problems. Participants who followed the new recommendations reduced the onset of serious complications from the disease by 50 to 60 percent. Some even managed to reverse mild kidney disease related to the illness.

With tens of thousands of people with diabetes trying to cope with the often devastating consequences of their illness, the new research findings are essential to their welfare. The project has been described by some experts as "the largest and most important study carried out in the history of diabetes." One researcher noted that while "the discovery of insulin was an absolute miracle—this study is in the ballpark of comparison."[3]

Although the research only involved those who had Type I diabetes, doctors feel the results may be useful for

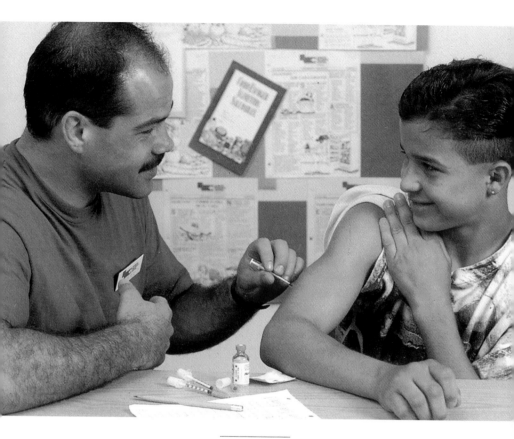

*With the help of insulin and proper
blood sugar monitoring, young people with
diabetes lead normal, active lives.*

individuals with Type II as well. That's because complications in both forms of the illness often develop for the
same reasons. Undoubtedly, the outlook for curing diabetes has brightened and physicians remain optimistic
about the future.

CHAPTER FIVE

Yes I Can

Being diabetic does not mean having to give up your hopes and dreams or settling for a lesser life in any way. There are countless success stories of young and old people with diabetes who accomplished what they set out to do, even though others believed the illness might stand in their way.

One such individual is 17-year-old Greg Smith. When Greg was 11 years old, his mother took him to the doctor for a routine check up. Although Greg didn't know it at the time, he was already displaying some of the classic signs of diabetes—weight loss, fatigue, hunger pangs, and a unquenchable thirst. But Greg had shrugged off his symptoms, and when he later learned that he had diabetes, he wanted to deny that, too.

Denial was Greg's first reaction. In time he overcame any obstacles diabetes might have posed by building on the positive aspects in his life. He described the process this way, "For one thing, facing up to my illness has helped me meet other difficulties head on. As I came to terms with my disease, I learned to take control, to pay attention to detail, to be responsible for my actions and their consequences. I've learned to manage my illness directly, instead of denying it, and that's made it easier to handle."[1]

Greg remained active, often throwing around a football with his father as well as playing soccer. Determined not to let diabetes hamper his athletic potential, Greg learned to plan ahead. He monitored his blood sugar and adjusted his food and insulin so he could participate in a broad range of sports. Besides eventually playing high-school football, Greg also ran track and played volleyball and basketball.

In assessing his drive and positive approach Greg noted, "I think because I had to learn to deal with diabetes when I was quite young, I realized that I didn't have to let things get me down. . . . In fact, I can use adversity to make myself a better person. I've learned a lot about myself—both from having diabetes and from playing football. When things get tough, I look inside, and decide whether I'm going to give up and say it's not worth it . . . or grit my teeth, and just do it. I've learned that I'm not a quitter, I'm pretty tough."[2]

Greg Smith is solid proof of what someone can accomplish despite having diabetes. With knowledge and effort, the possibilities are endless.

E N D
NOTES

CHAPTER 2

1. Gail Malesky, "Top Tips for Diabetic Self-Care," *Prevention*, September 1989, 74.

2. "Pregnancy Raises the Risk of Type II Diabetes," *Science News*, November 4, 1989, 294.

3. June Biermann and Barbara Toohey, The *Diabetic's Book* (Los Angeles: Jeremy P. Tarcher, 1990), 2.

CHAPTER 3

1. Diana Benzaia, "The Lifestyle Disease Only You Can Prevent," *Consumer's Digest*, June 1986, 49.

2. "High Fiber for Diabetics," *Saturday Evening Post*, January/February 1990, 12.

3. Ron Cowen, "Seeds of Protection," *Science News*, June 2, 1990, 351.

4. Gail Malesky, "Top Tips for Diabetic Self-Care," *Prevention*, September 1989, 74.

5. Ibid.

6. Ibid., 75

7. Ibid., 77

8. Ibid., 79

9. Luba Vikhanski, "Exercise Reduces Risk of Diabetes," *Medical World* News, July 1992, 7.

CHAPTER 4

1. Greg Gutfeld, "Disease-Free Disease?" *Prevention,* December 1992, 20.

2. Ibid.

3. Sandra Blakeslee, "Doctors Announce Ways to Forestall the Effects of Diabetes," *New York Times,* June 14, 1993, A12.

CHAPTER 5

1. Greg Smith, "Tackling Diabetes," *JFD International Countdown,* 4.

2. Ibid.

GLOSSARY

amputation—the removal of a limb through surgery

coma—a state of deep unconsciousness brought on by illness or injury

dialysis—the removal of toxic substances in the blood as the result of poor kidney function

glucose—a form of sugar created when starches and sugars are digested

heredity—a trait or condition passed on from one's parents or ancestors

hormone—a bodily secretion released into the bloodstream in small amounts by a gland or other tissue

hyperglycemia—also known as high blood sugar, this condition results from a buildup of glucose (sugar) in the bloodstream when there isn't enough insulin to use it

hypoglycemia—also known as low blood sugar, this condition results when a person's blood sugar level drops below normal. If the individual isn't speedily treated for it, he or she can become unconscious.

insulin—a substance released by specific cells in the pancreas, which is essential in turning digested foods into energy needed by the body

ketones—acids formed in the body when fats are broken down or digested

FURTHER
READING

Almonte, Paul, and Theresa Desmond. *Diabetes*. New York: Crestwood House, 1991.

Arneson, D. J. *Nutrition and Disease: Looking for the Link*. New York: Franklin Watts, 1992.

Curtis, Robert H., M.D. *Medicine*. New York: Scribner's, 1992.

Haines, Gail Kay. *Sugar Is Sweet*. New York: Atheneum, 1992.

Parker, Steve. *Food and Digestion*. New York: Franklin Watts, 1991.

Patent, Dorothy Hinshaw. *Nutrition: What's in the Food We Eat*. New York: Holiday House, 1992.

Ward, Brian. *Dieting and Good Eating*. New York: Franklin Watts, 1991.

Organizatons
Concerned with Diabetes

American Association of Diabetes Educators
500 N. Michigan Ave., Suite 1400
Chicago, IL 606121

American Diabetes Association
Diabetes Information Service Center
1660 Duke Street
Alexandria, VA 22314

Juvenile Diabetes Foundation International
The Diabetes Research Foundation
432 Park Avenue South
New York, NY 10016-8013

Juvenile Diabetes Foundation/Canada
4632 Yonge Street, Suite 100
Willowdale, Ontario
Canada M2N 5M1

Juvenile Diabetes Foundation/United Kingdom
8c Accmodation
London NW 11 8ED
England

INDEX